Thank you for choosing Jade Summer®.

Jade Summer® is a brand owned by Fritzen Publishing LLC, represents the work of multiple artists, and is registered in the U.S. Patent and Trademark Office.

Have a question? Please visit JadeSummer.com to learn more and send us a message.

We hope you have a great experience with this book and we appreciate your support.

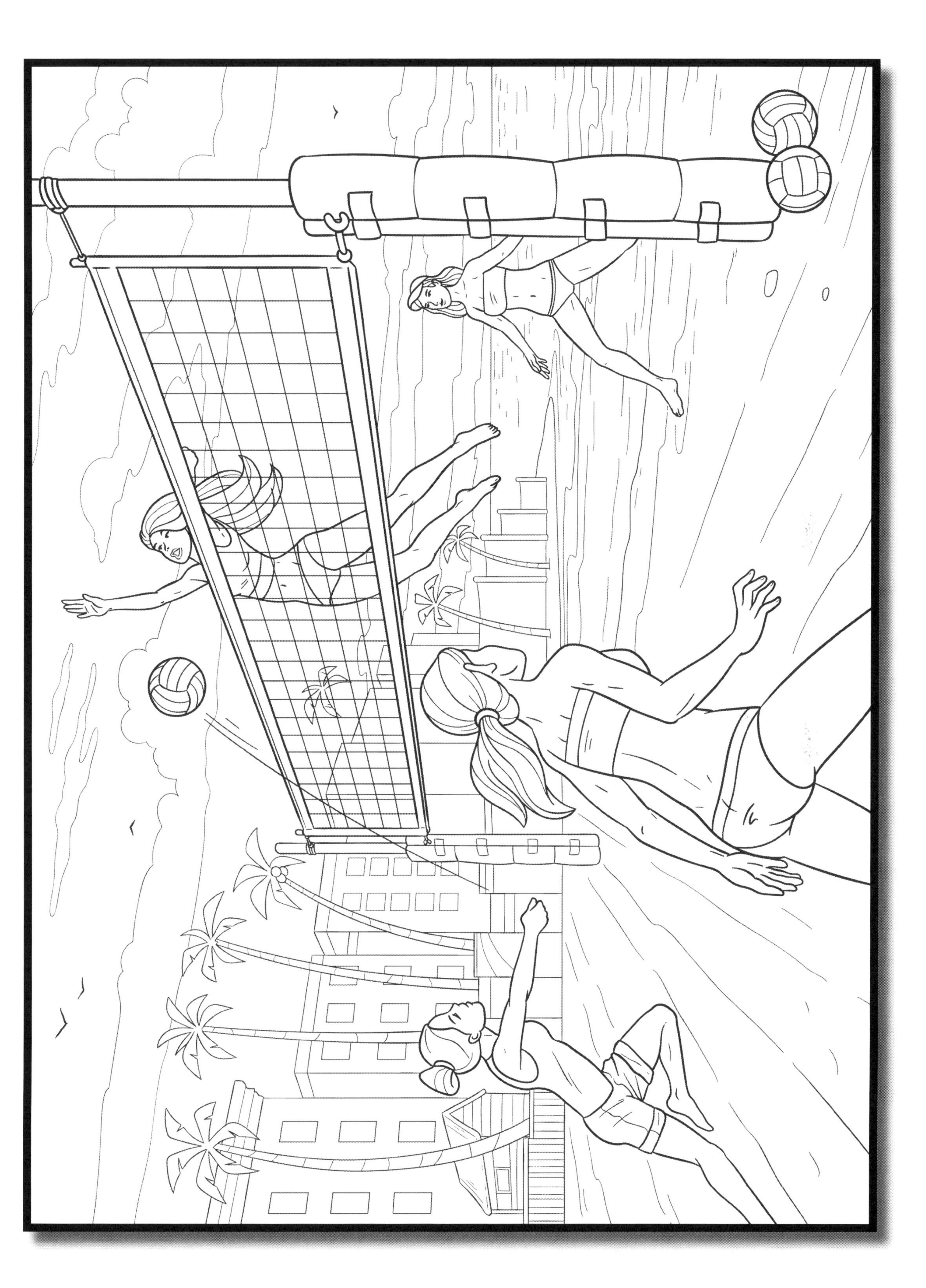

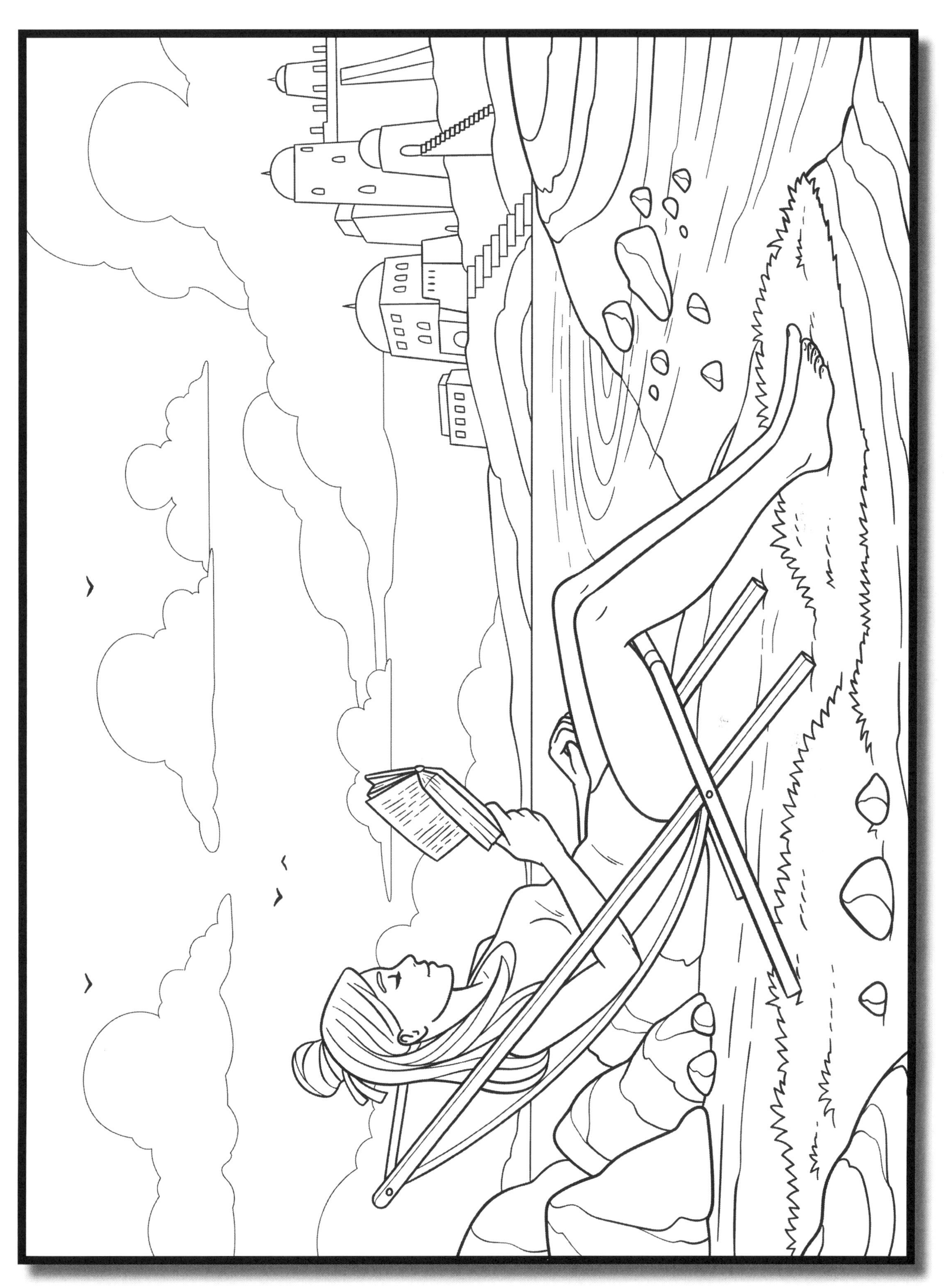

FIND YOUR NEXT BOOK ON JADESUMMER.COM

100 Amazing Patterns
100 Animals
100 Flowers
100 Magical Mandalas
100 Magical Patterns
100 Magical Swirls
Adorable Owls
Alice in Wonderland
Alice Grayscale
Animal Mandalas (2018)
Animals for Beginners
Anime
Art Nouveau
Autumn
Baby Dragons
Beach Homes
Beach Vacations
Beautiful Birds
Beautiful Flowers
Beginner Collection
Chibi Animals
Chibi Girls #1
Chibi Girls #2
Chibi Girls Grayscale
Chibi Girls Horror
Christmas #1
Christmas #2
Christmas #3
Christmas Animals
Christmas Flowers
Christmas Mandalas
Christmas Patterns
Color Charts
Costume Cats
Country Cabins
Country Cats
Country Farm
Country Romance
Cute Animals
Cute Animals #2
Cute Cats
Cute Christmas
Cute Fairies
Cute Fairies Grayscale
Cute Unicorns
Cute Witches
Dark Fantasy
Delicious Food
Dragons
Dreams Come True
Easter
Emoji
Fairies
Fairies Grayscale
Fantasy Adventure
Fantasy Collection #1
Fantasy Collection #2
Fantasy Grayscale
Fantasy Kids
Flower Bouquets
Flower Girls
Flower Mandalas
Flowers for Beginners
Forest Animals
Geometric Mandalas
Graffiti Animals
Greatest Hits (2019)
Greek Mythology
Halloween
Haunted House
Hidden Garden
Inspirational Collection
Inspirational Quotes
Inspirational Words
Interior Designs
Intricate Flowers
Intricate Mandalas
Kawaii Fantasy

Kawaii Girls
Kawaii Grayscale
Lazy Animals
Lazy Dogs
Light Fantasy
Live Your Dreams
Love
Magical Forest
Mandalas for Beginners
Masks
Mermaids
Mermaids (2018)
Mermaids Grayscale
Mini Mandalas
Mom Coloring Book
Nightmare
Oceans
Princesses
Proud to be a Girl
Psalms
Relaxing Flowers
Secret Jungle
Sloths
Springtime Animals
Springtime Flowers
Stained Glass Flowers #1
Stained Glass Flowers #2
Stuffed Animals
Sugar Skulls
Summer
Swirls for Beginners
Tattoos #1
Tattoos #2
Tattoos Grayscale
Unicorns #1
Unicorns #2
Unicorns Grayscale
Wonderful Christmas

BONUS PAGE
BEACH HOMES

Printed in Great Britain
by Amazon